PHILIP GROEBER
DAVID HOGE
REY SANCHEZ

EDITED BY
LEO WELCH

Contents

Production: Frank J. Hackinson
Production Coordinator: Philip Groeber
Cover Design/Illustrations: Terpstra Design, San Francisco
David B. Martin, Miami Beach
Cover Photo: courtesy of C.F. Martin Guitar & Co., Inc., Nazareth, PA
Text Editor: Pamela Hoge
Engraving: Tempo Music Press, Inc.
Printer: Tempo Music Press, Inc.

ISBN-13: 978-1-56939-649-0

FJH MUSIC COMPANY INC.
Frank J. Hackinson

REVIEW OF BOOK 2

Chords

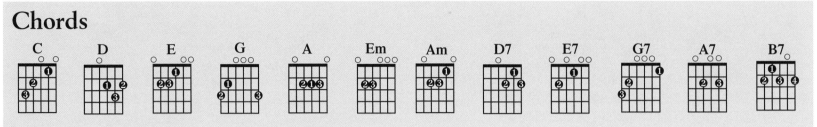

The student strums chords softly and evenly.
The teacher plays the melody throughout this book.

The More We Get Together

American Traditional

♩ = 92

The more we get to-geth-er, to-geth-er, to-geth-er; the more we get to-geth-er, the hap-pier we'll be! For your friends are my friends and my friends are your friends. The more we get to-geth-er the hap-pier we'll be!

continue strum pattern throughout

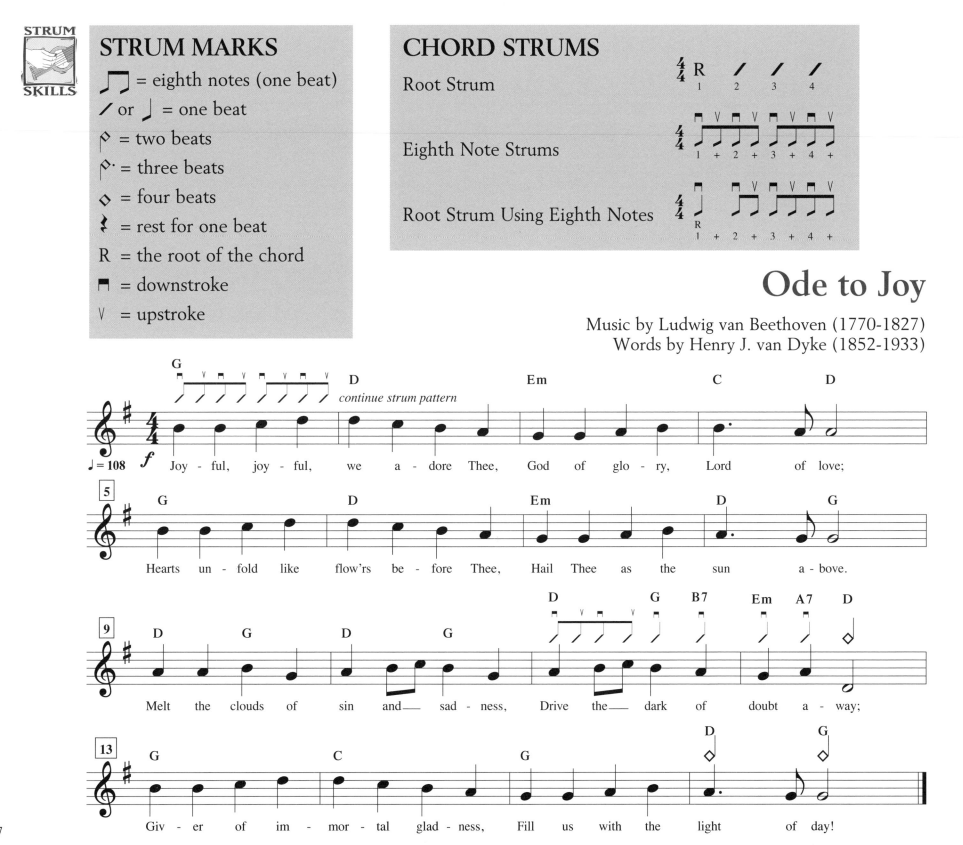

STRUM MARKS

♫ = eighth notes (one beat)

/ or ♩ = one beat

♩ = two beats

♩· = three beats

◇ = four beats

𝄽 = rest for one beat

R = the root of the chord

⊓ = downstroke

V = upstroke

CHORD STRUMS

Root Strum

Eighth Note Strums

Root Strum Using Eighth Notes

Ode to Joy

Music by Ludwig van Beethoven (1770-1827)
Words by Henry J. van Dyke (1852-1933)

continue strum pattern

♩ = 108 f

Joy - ful, joy - ful, we a - dore Thee, God of glo - ry, Lord of love;

Hearts un - fold like flow'rs be - fore Thee, Hail Thee as the sun a - bove.

Melt the clouds of sin and — sad - ness, Drive the — dark of doubt a - way;

Giv - er of im - mor - tal glad - ness, Fill us with the light of day!

TIES

- The use of a **tie** can help create a more interesting strum pattern.
- When two strums are tied, play the first strum only, allowing it to sound for the combined value of both strums.

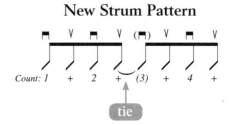

Worried Man Blues

 When learning the new strum pattern on this page, you will see a downstroke symbol (⊓) in parentheses. Your strumming hand should go through the motion of a downstroke *without* actually playing the strings. This will apply to upstrokes (V) in parentheses as well.

4

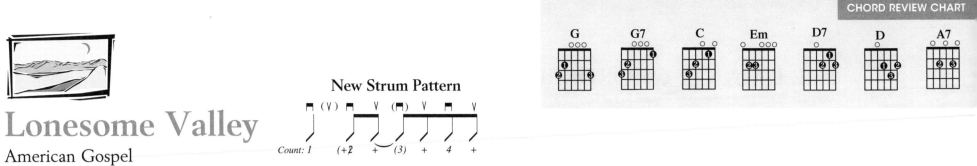

Lonesome Valley

American Gospel

New Strm Pattern

Count: 1 (+2 + (3) + 4 +

- Once you have learned the strum pattern, play with enthusiasm to add excitement to the song!
- A very soulful arrangement of this song occurs in the movie *O Brother, Where Art Thou?*

continue strum pattern throughout

♩ = 104

You've got to walk_____ that lone - some val - ley,_____ you got to

walk_____ it by your - self._____ ain't no - bod - y

here_____ can walk it for you._____ You got to

walk that lone - some val - ley by your - self._____

When listening to recordings, pay close attention to the guitar accompaniment. Here is a partial list of some great guitar performers: Chuck Berry, The Carter Family, Bob Dylan, Joni Mitchell, Pete Seeger, Paul Simon, Bruce Springsteen, James Taylor, and many others.

THE F MAJOR CHORD (F)

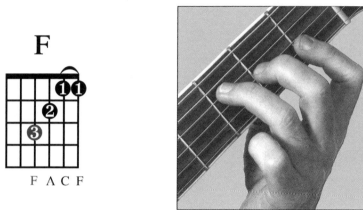

F

F A C F

The F chord uses a **barre** in which one finger holds down two strings.

- First practice the F chord without using the first finger. This will help you to get your hand and arm into a good position.

- Add the first finger as shown in the photograph above. Notice that you will be pressing somewhat on the side of your first finger. Your left elbow should be slightly tucked in toward your side.

- Practice the F chord *without left-hand pressure* at first. When you press down, keep a relaxed look in your hand and arm.

TECHNIQUE TIP The F chord can be challenging at first. Be patient, practicing this chord a little each day. Learning to play *barre* chords will allow you to be able to play chord accompaniment to almost any song!

Note to the teacher and student: Because the F chord has no open strings and is **movable**, you may begin playing the F chord on higher frets, which makes getting a good sound a little easier.

PRIMARY CHORDS IN THE KEY OF C MAJOR

New Strum Pattern

Oh, Mary Don't You Weep

American Folksong

Oh, Ma - ry don't you weep, don't you mourn. Oh, Ma - ry don't you weep, don't you mourn.

Phar - aoh's ar - my got drowned, Oh, Ma - ry don't you weep.

Primary Chords

Music of the past several hundred years has been mostly based on three **primary chords**. Although songs can use many chords, the primary chords are the most important. They are often referred to as the I, IV, and V chords. These numbers refer to their location in the major scale.

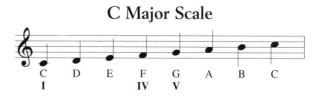

C Major Scale

PRIMARY CHORDS IN THE KEY OF G MAJOR

Old Dan Tucker

American Folksong

Bruce Springsteen recorded this song in 2006 on the CD
We Shall Overcome: The Seeger Sessions.

MUSIC MASTER

RHYTHM REMINDER: When strumming patterns that use ties, your right hand should continue to move down (⊓) and up (∨), even though you need to "miss" the strings when a tie appears.

New Strum Pattern

Count: 1 + 2 + 3 + 4 +

Come Back Liza

Jamaican Folksong

♩ = 96

Ev - 'ry time I 'mem - ber Li - za, wa - ter come___ a me eye.

continue strum pattern throughout

Ev - 'ry time I think 'bout Li - za, wa - ter come___ a me eye.

Come back, Li - za, come back gal,___ wa - ter come___ a me eye.

Come back Li - za, come back gal,___ wa - ter come___ a me eye.

STRUM SKILLS

Sometimes you may want to add an extra strum at the end of a piece in order to hear a final ending.

wa - ter come___ a me eye.

POWER CHORDS

- **Power chords** are used in many popular and rock songs.

- They consist of only two notes: the **root** of the chord and the **fifth** of the chord.

- They are often played with distortion on electric guitars. The unique sound of power chords makes them fun to play.

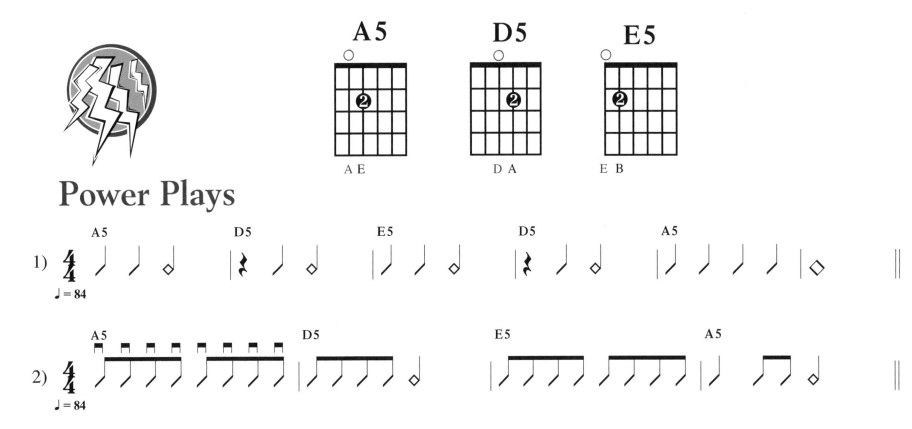

Power Plays

The lowest-pitched note of power chords will almost always be the root.
Power chords are usually played using only downstrokes.
With practice, you will learn to play the two strings accurately
(without striking other strings).

- Some power chords are movable because there are no open strings, such as F5.

- With this chord shape, your first finger will always play the root, and your third finger will always play the fifth.

- Keep the left-hand fingers spread out to make it easier to play this chord.

F5

FC

Erie Canal

Thomas S. Allen
(1876-1919)

First and Second Endings
Play the first ending and then repeat. Then play the second ending, skipping over the first ending.

TABLATURE

- Guitar music is often written in **tablature** (TAB), a centuries-old notation system.

- The strings are represented by six horizontal lines; the top line is the first string. Numbers indicate which frets to play.

- The use of tablature can make guitar music easier to understand. Generally, there are no rhythms indicated in tablature. The melody to *Old McDonald* is an example of music written in single note tablature.

Old McDonald

American Folksong

- The use of tablature makes it easier to read music that looks difficult, as in *Ritchie's Song*.

Ritchie's Song

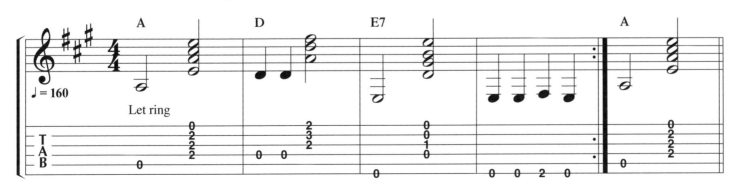

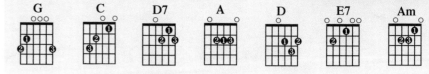

ROOT AND FIFTH STRUM

- Another bass note to add to the Root Strum is the **fifth** of the chord.
- You can quickly find the fifth by counting on your fingers.
- The fifth may be a higher pitch or a lower pitch than the root.

Here is a chart of some of the roots and fifths you will use in this book.

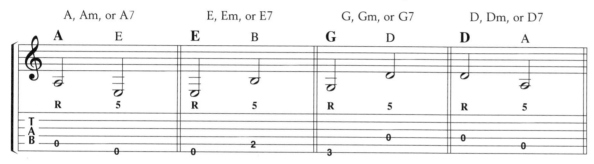

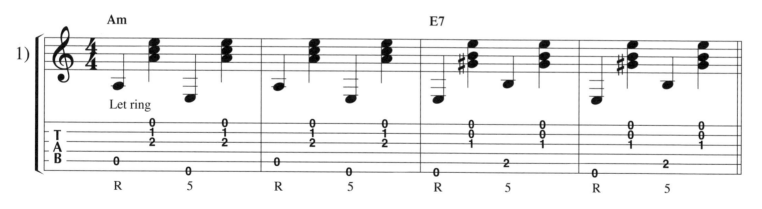

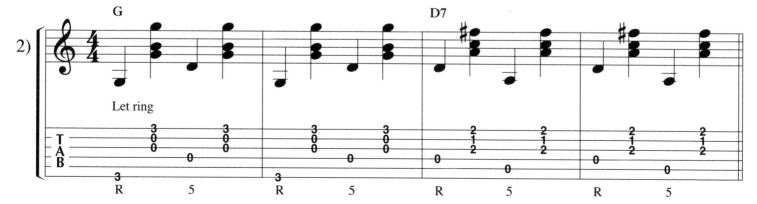

PRIMARY CHORDS IN THE KEY OF A MINOR

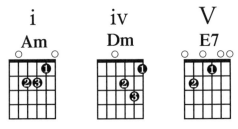

A la nanita nana

Traditional Spanish Carol

A la na - ni - ta na - na na na - ni - ta na - na, na - ni - ta e - a.

Mi Je - sus tie - ne sue - no, ben - di - to se - a ben - di - to se - a.

When playing the Root and Fifth Strum, be sure to let the notes ring out as long as possible.

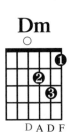

D minor (Dm) is a new chord.

14

PRIMARY CHORDS IN THE KEY OF E MINOR

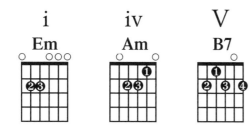

Adelita

Francisco Tárrega
(1852-1909)
(arranged)

continue strum pattern throughout

Francisco Tárrega was a famous Spanish guitarist
who composed many pieces for the classical guitar.

When Johnny Comes Marching Home Again

Louis Lambert
(1829-1892)

This song dates back to the Civil War. It is one of the few patriotic songs written in a minor key. The lyrics, by Irish American bandleader Patrick S. Gilmore, were published under the pen name of Louis Lambert.

America, the Beautiful

Music by Samuel A. Ward (1847-1903)
Words by Katharine L. Bates (1859-1929)

continue strum pattern throughout

O beau - ti - ful for spa - cious skies, for am - ber waves of grain, For

pur - ple moun - tain maj - es - ties a - bove the fruit - ed plain! A -

mer - i - ca! A - mer - i - ca! God shed His grace on thee, And

crown thy good with broth - er - hood from sea to shin - ing sea.

There are optional versions of many chords.
This new E7 chord adds another D note which
gives the chord a different sound.

E7

E B D G# D E

PRIMARY CHORDS IN THE KEY OF D MAJOR

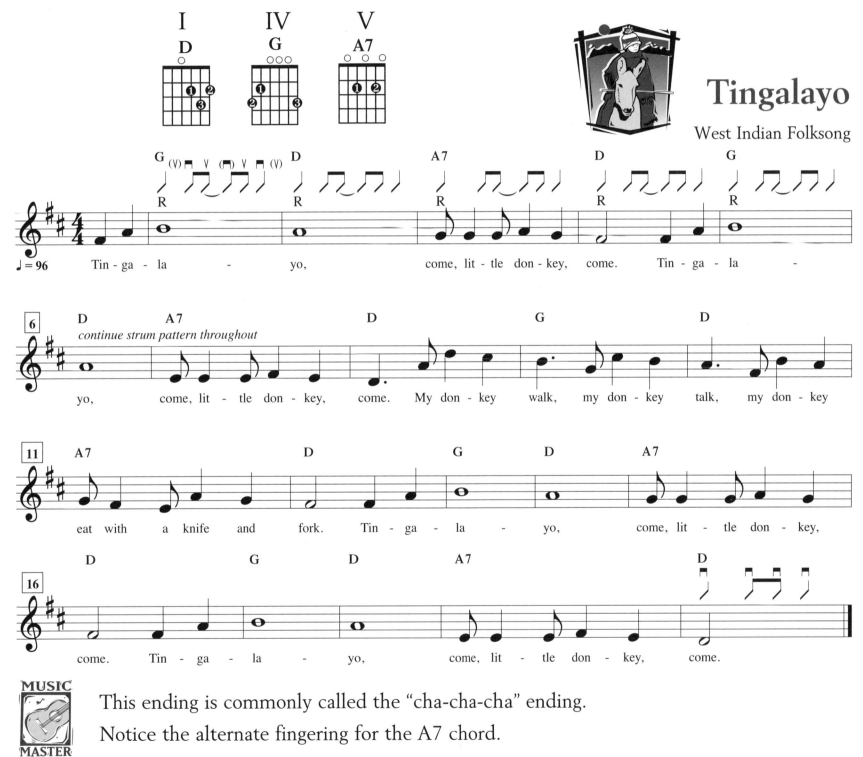

Tingalayo

West Indian Folksong

This ending is commonly called the "cha-cha-cha" ending.

Notice the alternate fingering for the A7 chord.

My Bonnie

Scottish Folksong

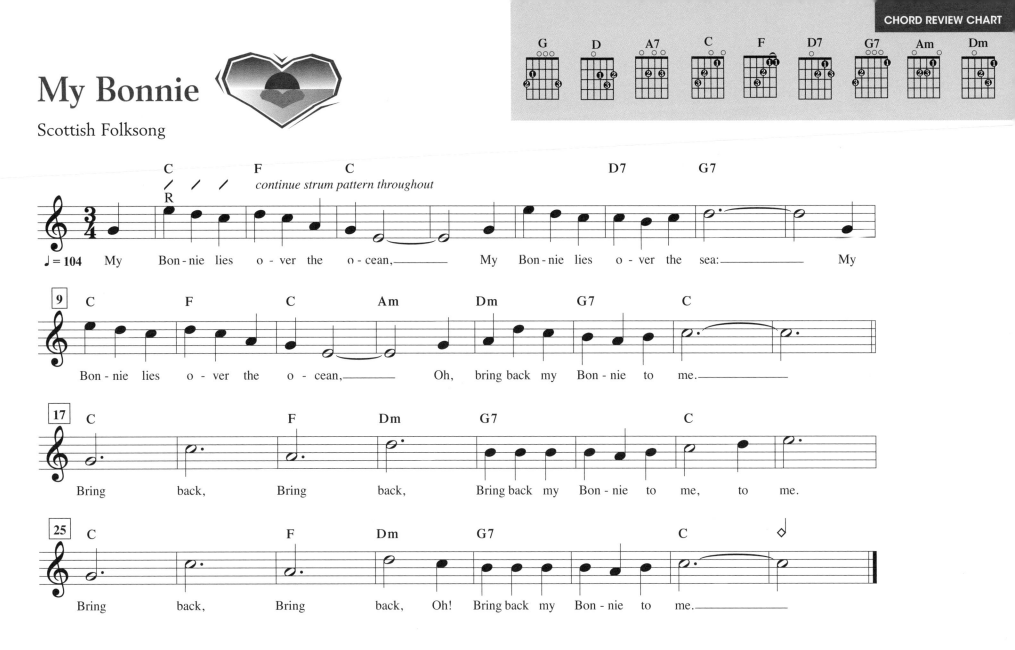

When playing the Root Strum pattern, it is okay to place and play the root notes before placing the rest of the fingers of the chord.

My Bonnie was one of the first songs ever recorded by The Beatles.

37

THE CAPO

- A **capo** is a clamping device that holds all six strings down on any given fret, raising the pitch of the open strings by one half step for every fret. For example, a capo placed on the first fret will make an E chord sound like an F, an A chord sound like a B♭, etc.

- You can use a capo to place a song in a comfortable key for singing, or to simplify a key that has many difficult chords. See page 38 for more information on how to use a capo.

- Capos are inexpensive, yet valuable for any guitarist.

Happy Birthday to You

Words by Mildred J. Hill and Patty S. Hill
Music Traditional

Capo the 2nd fret (Key of E major)

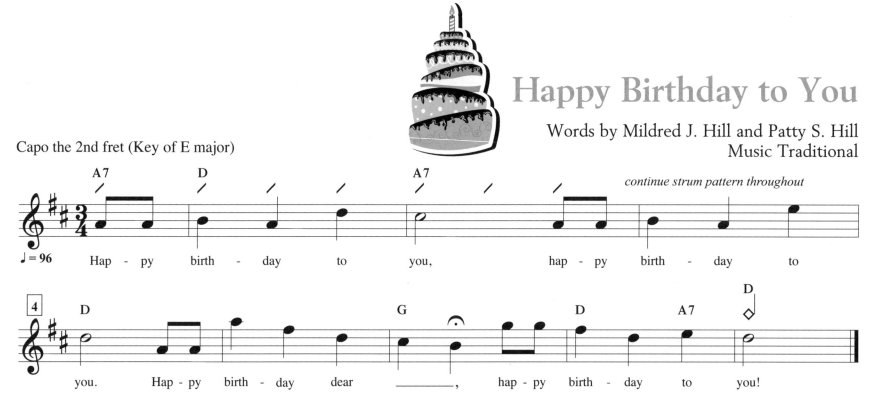

continue strum pattern throughout

A7   D   A7

♩ = 96   Hap - py birth - day to you, hap - py birth - day to

D   G   D   A7   D

you. Hap - py birth - day dear _____, hap - py birth - day to you!

The symbol (⌒) is a **_fermata_**, which means you may hold this chord (or note) as long as you want.

Happy Birthday to You is the most often performed song of all time!

Skip to My Lou

American Folksong

Capo the 5th fret (Key of D major)

Flies in the but-ter-milk, shoo, fly, shoo! Flies in the but-ter-milk, shoo, fly, shoo!

Flies in the but-ter-milk, shoo, fly, shoo! Skip to my Lou, my dar - ling!

Skip, skip, skip to my Lou, skip, skip, skip to my Lou,

Skip, skip, skip to my Lou, skip to my Lou, my dar - ling!

Ear Training

Play *Skip to My Lou* without looking at the music. Rely on your ears to tell you when to change chords. Try this new skill on other songs in this book, such as *The More We Get Together* (page 2) and *Worried Man Blues* (page 4). Ear training is a very important skill for all musicians.

FINGERSTYLE (or FINGERPICKING)

- The right-hand thumb and fingers are often used to pluck the strings.

- Follow the right-hand position indicated in the photos very carefully. The proper position is very important in **fingerstyle** accompaniment.

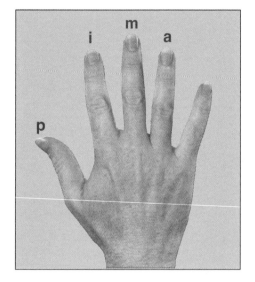

- Each finger has a letter name derived from the Spanish word.

    p = *pulgar* (thumb)
    i = *indice* (index)
    m = *media* (middle)
    a = *anular* (ring)

- Position your right hand towards the midpoint between the bridge and the fingerboard, or the edge of the soundhole.

- The wrist should be aligned naturally with the hand and forearm.

- The fingers (*i*, *m*, and *a*) should be held in a relaxed curve, as if you are holding a bubble.

- The thumb (*p*) is extended slightly, allowing the thumb and fingers to play without bumping into each other.

- The nails may be used to help produce a louder and more beautiful sound. File your nails so that they pass smoothly over the strings.

MUSIC MASTER

An **arpeggio** is when notes of a chord are played one after another (instead of at the same time). Fingerstyle accompaniments often use arpeggios (as in *My Grandfather's Clock* on page 23).

THE FREE STROKE

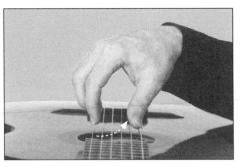

- Place (*or prepare*) the fingertip on the string. Play the string with a "scratching" motion, moving mostly from the knuckle.

- When playing free strokes, your finger will pass *freely* above the adjacent string (without touching it).

- Place (*or prepare*) the thumb on the string.

- Play the string with a forward and upward motion.

- Your thumb will pass *freely* above the adjacent string.

- Use free strokes when fingerpicking chords.

Some songs will have the right-hand accompaniment pattern written in TAB.

My Grandfather's Clock

Henry Clay Work (1832-1884)

Santa Lucia

Neapolitan Boat Song

- When playing the accompaniment for *Santa Lucia*, you will be using *i*, *m*, and *a* together. A chord played in this way is called a **block chord**.

- When playing three notes together, try to make it feel as if you are using one large finger.

Fingerstyle

♩ = 92

Now 'neath the sil-ver moon, o-cean is glow-ing. O'er the calm bil-low,
Sul ma - re luc-ci-a, l'as-tro d'ar-gen-to. Pla-ci-da è l'on-da,

soft winds are blow-ing. Who then will sail with me, in my boat
pros-p ro è il ven-to. Ve-ni-te al-l'a-agi-le bar-chet-ta

o'er the sea? San-ta Lu-ci-a! San-ta Lu-ci-a!
mi-a... San-ta Lu-ci-a! San-ta Lu-ci-a!

24

Oh, My Darling Clementine

American Folksong

- This fingerpicking pattern is similar to the one on page 24, with the addition of roots and fifths.
- When playing the C chord, your third finger must move over to G on the sixth string to play the fifth.

Fingerstyle

♩ = 100

In a cav - ern, in a can - yon, ex - ca - vat - ing for a mine, Dwelt a min - er, for - ty -

nin - er, and his daugh - ter Clem-en - tine. Oh, my dar - ling, oh, my dar - ling, oh, my

dar - ling Clem-en - tine; You are lost and gone for - ev - er, dread-ful sor - ry, Clem-en - tine.

SLASH CHORDS

- A **slash chord** is a chord in which the lowest-pitched note is *not* the root.

- These chords are notated with two letters separated by a slash (see G/F♯ in the example below). The first letter is the name of the chord. The second letter is the name of the bass note to be played.

- Slash chords create interesting new sounds for chord accompaniments; and can provide a smooth transition between bass notes (lower-pitched notes) when changing from one chord to the next.

Fingerpicking Good!

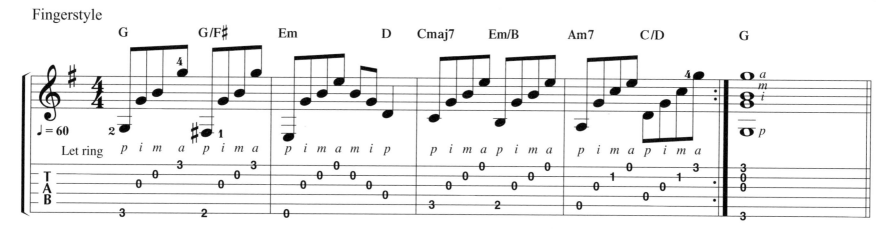

Popular songs may use many slash chords. It is not always necessary to include the bass note indicated, especially when playing along with other performers. With practice, you will become more comfortable with playing slash chords.

Auld Lang Syne

Traditional Scottish Melody
Words by Robert Burns (1759-1796)

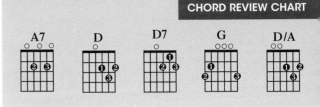

CHORD REVIEW CHART

• Most songs may be played with a pick or fingerpicking. Experiment with both styles.

Should auld ac-quaint-ance be for-got, And nev-er brought to mind? Should

auld ac-quaint-ance be for-got, And days of auld lang syne! For

auld____ lang____ syne, my dear, For auld____ lang____ syne. We'll

take a cup o' kind - ness yet, For days of auld lang syne.

Auld Lang Syne has traditionally been played on New Year's Eve. Guy Lombardo and his "Royal Canadians" performed it annually on a radio show for many years. The title of this song of friendship is written in Scottish dialect, which translates to "Old Long Since."

Sloop John B.

Traditional

Watch for the slash chords in measures 10 and 13.

Play the "cha-cha-cha" ending for this song!

Sloop John B. was recorded by The Beach Boys.

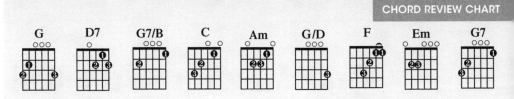

Michael, Row the Boat Ashore

Traditional American

♩ = 96

1.☐Mi - chael, row the boat a - shore, Al - le - lu -
helped to trim the sail, Al - le - lu -

4 continue strum pattern throughout

ia! Mi - chael, row the boat a - shore, Al - le -
ia! Sis - ter helped to trim the sail, Al - le -

1. **7**
lu - ia! 2.☐Sis - ter

2.
lu - ia!

This traditional song has always been a favorite of guitarists.

Take Me Out to the Ball Game

Music by Albert Von Tilzer (1878-1956)
Words by Jack Norworth (1879-1959)

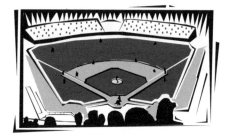

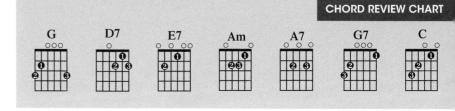

When Irish Eyes are Smiling

Music by Ernest R. Ball (1878-1927)
Words by Chauncey Olcott (1858-1932) and George Graff, Jr. (1886-1973)

037

Battle Hymn of the Republic

Civil War Song
Music by William Steffe (1830-1890)
Words by Julia Ward Howe (1819-1910)

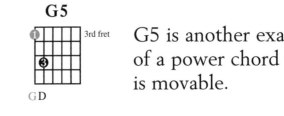

G5 is another example of a power chord that is movable.

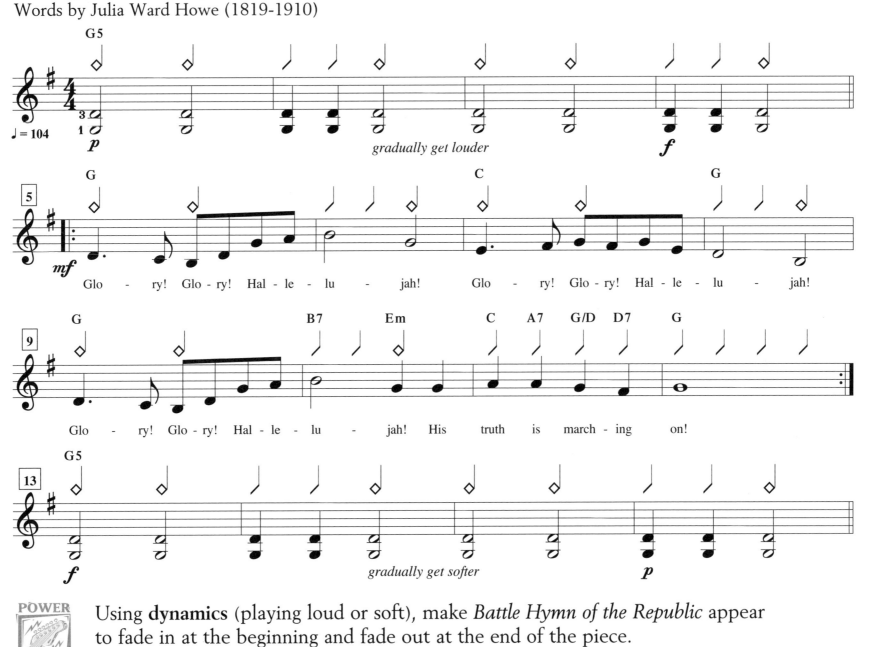

Glo - ry! Glo - ry! Hal - le - lu - jah! Glo - ry! Glo - ry! Hal - le - lu - jah!

Glo - ry! Glo - ry! Hal - le - lu - jah! His truth is march - ing on!

Using **dynamics** (playing loud or soft), make *Battle Hymn of the Republic* appear to fade in at the beginning and fade out at the end of the piece.

p = *piano*, soft   *mf* = *mezzo forte*, medium loud   *f* = *forte*, loud

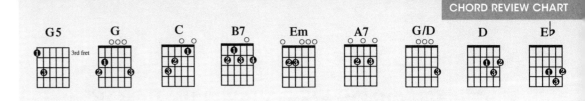

CHORD REWARD

- Movable chords (chords with no open strings) make it easy to play chords on different frets.

- The following song, *Reveille*, can be played on any fret you choose. Two examples are given.

Reveille

United States Bugle Call

- Now move one fret higher. Play on higher frets also.

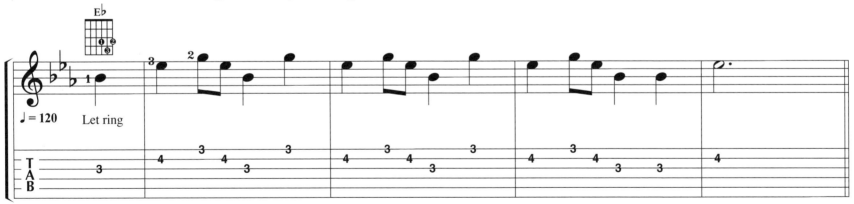

Reveille is the first call in the morning used to wake up the soldiers.

You may use a first-finger barre when playing the D and E♭ chords.

CHORDS USED IN THIS BOOK

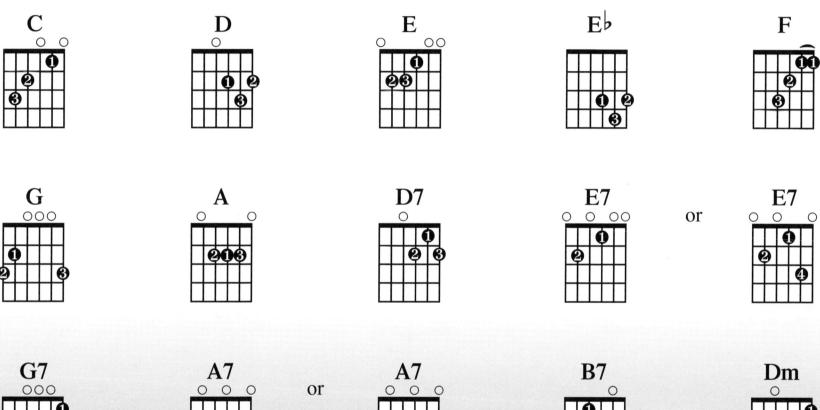

C   D   E   E♭   F

G   A   D7   E7   or   E7

G7   A7   or   A7   B7   Dm

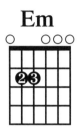 Em

 Am

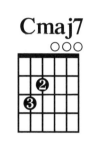 Am7

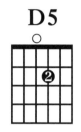 Cmaj7

D5

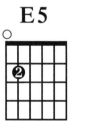 E5

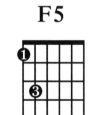 F5

G5 3rd fret

A5

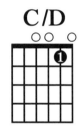 C/D

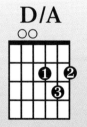 D/A

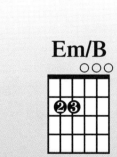 Em/B

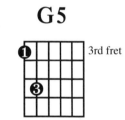 G7/B

G/D

 G/F♯

ACCOMPANIMENT PATTERNS

$\frac{4}{4}$ TIME

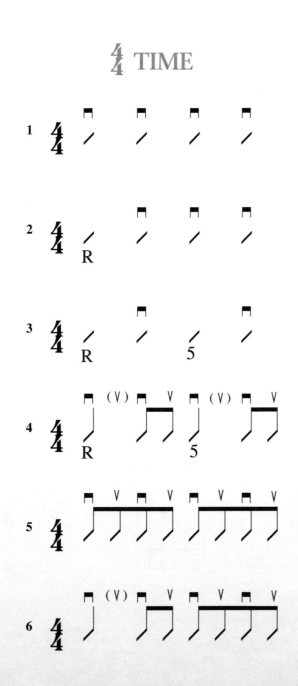

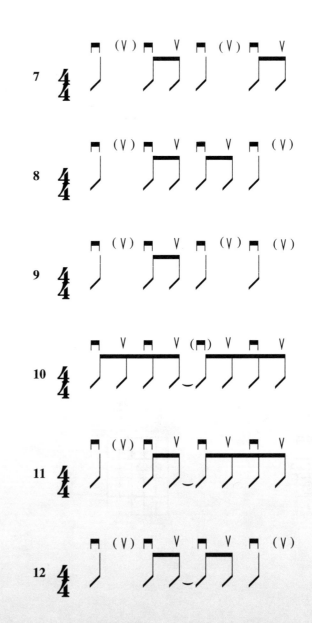

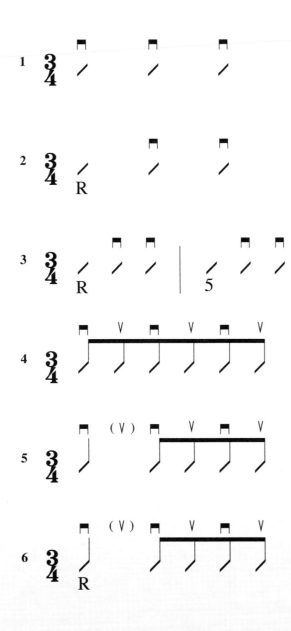

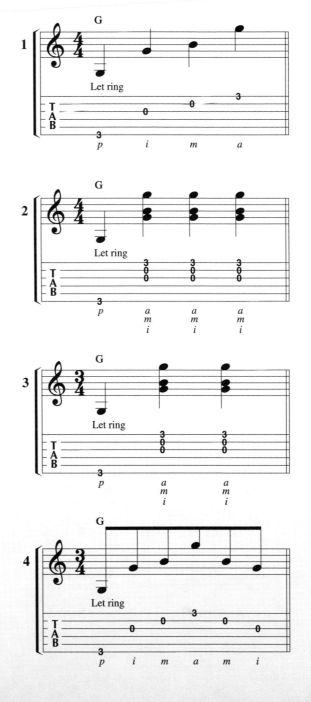

HOW TO USE A CAPO

- A capo may be used to change the key of a song for a more comfortable singing range.
- The following chart will help you play in common "guitar" keys while the guitar sounds in another.

CAPO THIS FRET ↓	PLAY IN THESE GUITAR KEYS				
	A	C	D	E	G
	CAPOED GUITAR SOUNDS IN THESE KEYS				
1	B♭ (or A♯)	D♭ (or C♯)	E♭ (or D♯)	F	A♭ (or G♯)
2	B	D	E	G♭ (or F♯)	A
3	C	E♭ (or D♯)	F	G	B♭ (or A♯)
4	D♭ (or C♯)	E	G♭ (or F♯)	A♭ (or G♯)	B
5	D	F	G	A	C
6	E♭ (or D♯)	G♭ (or F♯)	A♭ (or G♯)	B♭ (or A♯)	D♭ (or C♯)
7	E	G	A	B	D
8	F	A♭ (or G♯)	B♭ (or A♯)	C	E♭ (or D♯)
9	G♭ (or F♯)	A	B	D♭ (or C♯)	E
10	G	B♭ (or A♯)	C	D	F
11	A♭ (or G♯)	B	D♭ (or C♯)	E♭ (or D♯)	G♭ (or F♯)

GLOSSARY

SIGN	TERM	DEFINITION
	arpeggio	Playing the notes of a chord one at a time, not simultaneously.
	barre	A left-hand finger holds down two or more notes.
	block chord	A fingerpicking style in which the notes of a chord are sounded at once (as opposed to an arpeggio).
	capo	A clamping device that helps guitarists to change keys easily.
	dynamics	Symbols that indicate how loud or soft to play. p = *piano*, soft mf = *mezzo forte*, medium loud f = *forte*, loud
⌢	**fermata**	Indicates that a note or a rest should be held longer than usual.
5	**fifth**	The fifth letter name of a scale.
	Let ring	Allow the notes to sound as long as possible.
	major scale	Notes in alphabetical order using the following pattern of whole steps (W) and half steps (H). W W H W W W H
N.C.	**No chord**	Do not strum until chord symbols reappear.
	power chords	Two-note chords that use the root (R) and fifth (5) only.
	primary chords	The most commonly used chords in music. These chords are identified using Roman Numerals: I, IV, and V.
R	**root note**	The letter name of the chord.
G/D	**slash chord**	A chord in which the lowest-pitched note is not the root. G/D is a G chord with a D as the lowest-pitched note.

The FJH Young Beginner Guitar Method and Supplemental Material

The FJH Young Beginner Guitar Method is a well-conceived, graded guitar method designed especially for the younger beginner. Presenting one concept at a time, the method engages students with lively songs instead of exercises. Both teacher and student will enjoy the music right from the beginning! Adaptable in pick style or classical technique.

There are five publications in each of the three levels:
Lesson, Theory-Activity, Performance, Exploring Chords, and Christmas.

Level 1
Includes a pre-reading section that allows the student to play songs by reading fret numbers only. Natural notes in first position on strings one, two, and three are presented, along with basic rhythms. Dynamics are also introduced to develop musicianship at an early level. Includes optional teacher duets with chord names. Rhythmic accuracy is stressed throughout the method.

Level 2
Chords are introduced along with the natural notes on strings four, five, and six. New concepts include eighth notes, chromatics (sharps, flats and naturals), pick-up notes, ties, and rests. Students are encouraged to strum chords to accompany the melody whenever possible. Many optional teacher duets are included. (Students may enjoy playing the teacher duet parts as well!)

Level 3
In Lesson Book 3 the students learn complete chords with many opportunities to strum while the teacher plays the melody. New concepts include: dotted quarter notes, hammer-ons and pull-offs, major and minor pentatonic scales, major key theory and major scales, power chords, palm mute, solo styles, and music in Second Position. Music styles include popular, rock 'n' roll, blues, classics, multi-cultural, and music from various eras.

After the completion of Young Beginner Level 3 students move into **Everybody's Guitar Method**: **G1025 Book 1** if a review is needed; **G1030 Book 2** is the usual choice; **G1048** combines both Books 1 and 2 using tablature.

GuitarTime Series Christmas
G1001 Primer Level Pick Style
G1002 Level 1 Pick Style
G1003 Level 2 Pick Style
G1004 Level 3 Pick Style
G1005 Level 1 Classical Style
G1006 Level 2 Classical Style

GuitarTime Series Popular Folk
G1007 Primer Level Pick Style
G1008 Level 1 Pick Style
G1009 Level 2 Pick Style
G1010 Level 3 Pick Style
G1011 Level 1 Classical Style
G1012 Level 2 Classical Style

Everybody's Series
G1026 Flash Cards
G1029 Basic Guitar Chords
G1032 Basic Guitar Scales
G1042 Strum & Play Guitar Chords
G1043 Guitar Ensembles
G1049 Ukulele Method 1

Other Publications
G1058 My First Easy To Play Guitar TAB Book
G1060 My First Easy To Play Guitar Scale Book
G1061 My First Easy To Play Guitar Chord Book
G1059 The Big & Easy Songbook for Guitar with Tablature

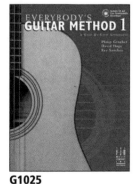

G1025

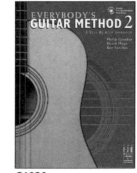

G1030

G1048